The Ancient Civilization of the Indus River

Indus Civilization Grade 4 | Children's Ancient History

BABY PROFESSOR
EDUCATION KIDS

First Edition, 2020

Published in the United States by Speedy Publishing LLC, 40 E Main Street, Newark, Delaware 19711 USA.

© 2020 Baby Professor Books, an imprint of Speedy Publishing LLC

Baby Professor Books are available at special discounts when purchased in bulk for industrial and sales-promotional use. For details contact our Special Sales Team at Speedy Publishing LLC, 40 E Main Street, Newark, Delaware 19711 USA. Telephone (888) 248-4521 Fax: (210) 519-4043.

10 9 8 7 6 * 5 4 3 2 1

Print Edition: 9781541953550
Digital Edition: 9781541956551
Hardcover Edition: 9781541977105

See the world in pictures. Build your knowledge in style.
www.speedypublishing.com

Table of Contents

INDUS RIVER AND VALLEY IN KARAKORAM, PAKISTAN

4

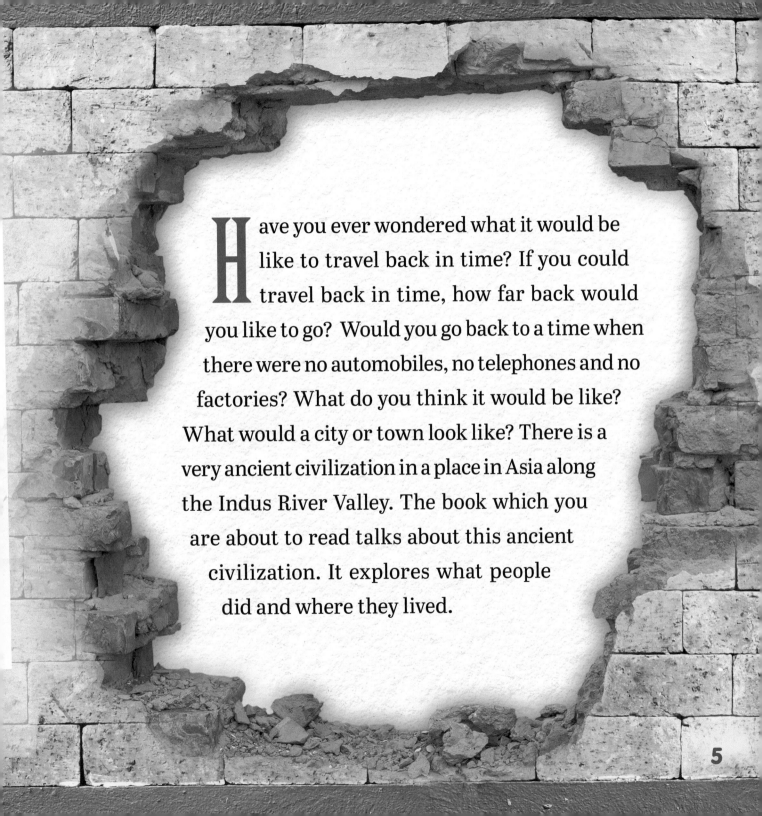

Have you ever wondered what it would be like to travel back in time? If you could travel back in time, how far back would you like to go? Would you go back to a time when there were no automobiles, no telephones and no factories? What do you think it would be like? What would a city or town look like? There is a very ancient civilization in a place in Asia along the Indus River Valley. The book which you are about to read talks about this ancient civilization. It explores what people did and where they lived.

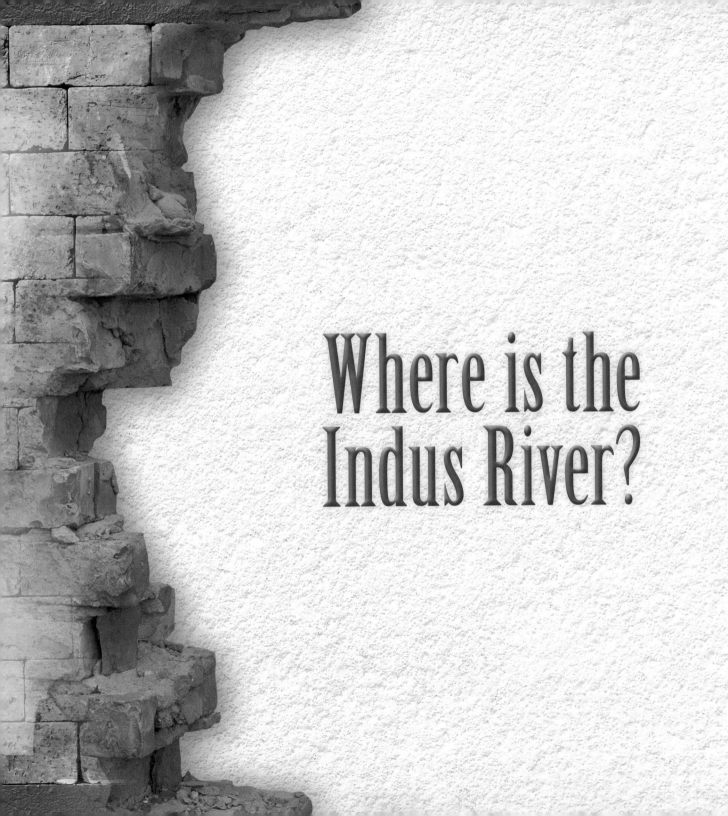

Where is the
Indus River?

The Indus River lies between Pakistan and India, two countries in Asia. The river starts in the Himalayas, a mountain range in which the highest mountain in the world, Mount Everest is located, until it reaches the Arabian Sea.

MOUNT EVEREST

THE INDUS RIVER LIES BETWEEN PAKISTAN AND INDIA.

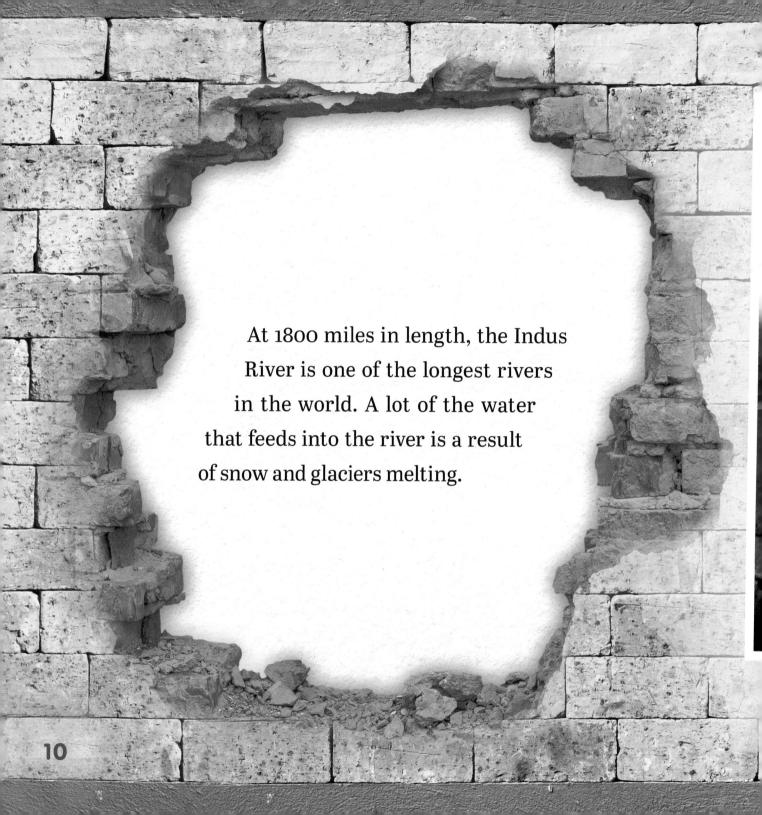

At 1800 miles in length, the Indus River is one of the longest rivers in the world. A lot of the water that feeds into the river is a result of snow and glaciers melting.

INDUS RIVER

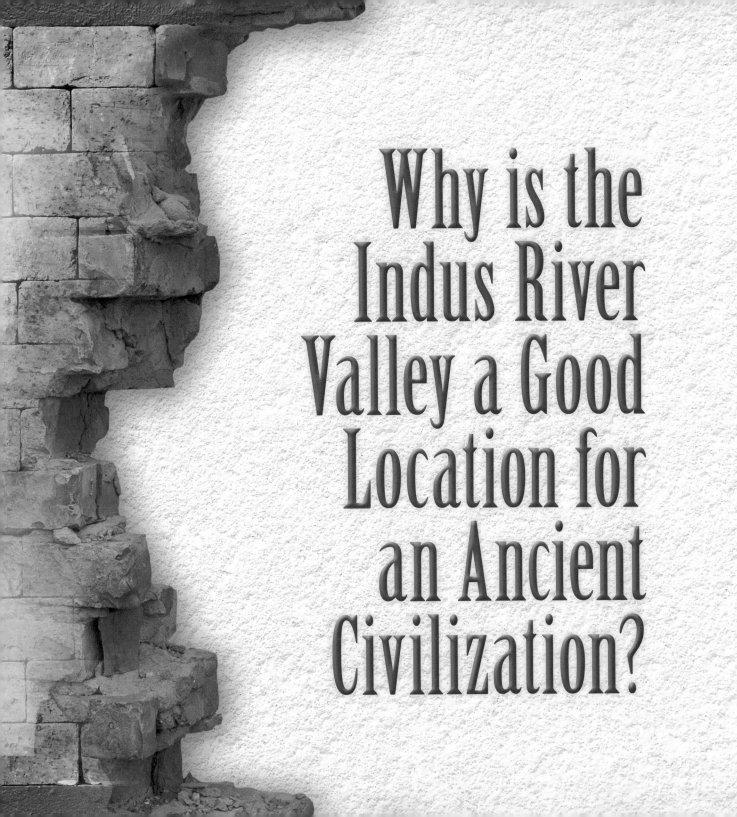

Why is the Indus River Valley a Good Location for an Ancient Civilization?

RIVERS PROVIDE FISH WHICH ARE COMMON AND HEALTHY FOOD SOURCE.

If we look at ancient civilizations, we can see that rivers have always been important to people and the communities in which the people have lived. There are many ways in which rivers prove to be very useful for people. They provide water for drinking, bathing, and farming. Rivers provide fish which are a common and healthy food source.

FISHING COMMUNITIES WITH THEIR HOUSEBOATS ALONG THE BANKS OF THE LOWER REACHES OF THE RIVER INDUS, PUNJAB, PAKISTAN.

IRRIGATED FARMLAND ALONG THE INDUS RIVER

Water is essential for human life. It is also not uncommon for civilizations to be found near valleys, as the rivers running down from the mountains contain mixtures of silt. This material helps to make the soil fertile. Along with seasonal flooding, it allows for good ground from which crops can be grown.

It is no surprise, therefore, that the Indus Valley could become the site of one of the earliest civilizations known. It is even from the word Indus that the country India came to be named. The Indus River was so significant in the lives of the ancient people that the hymns from ancient India even talk about it.

INDUS VALLEY

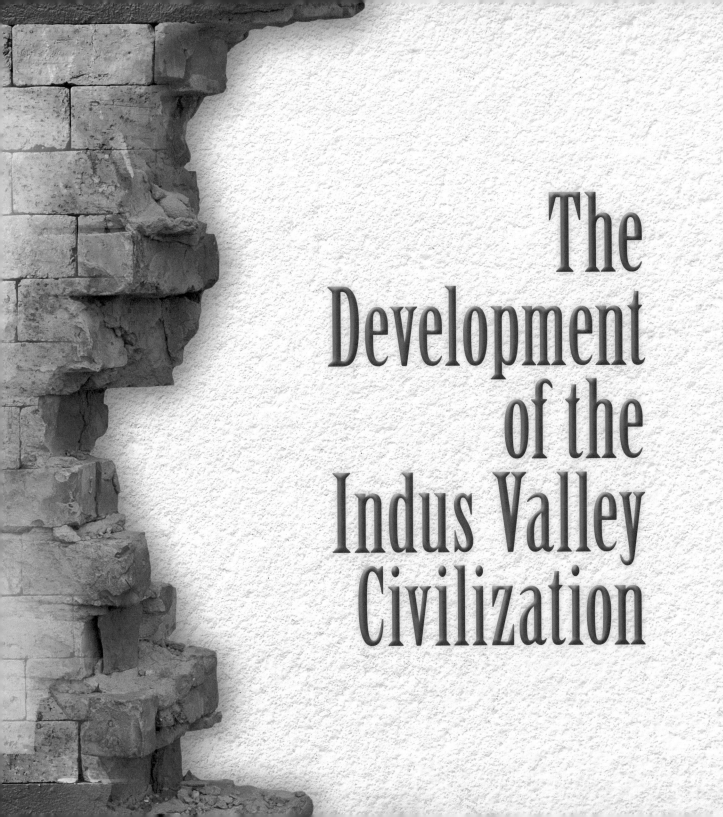

The
Development
of the
Indus Valley
Civilization

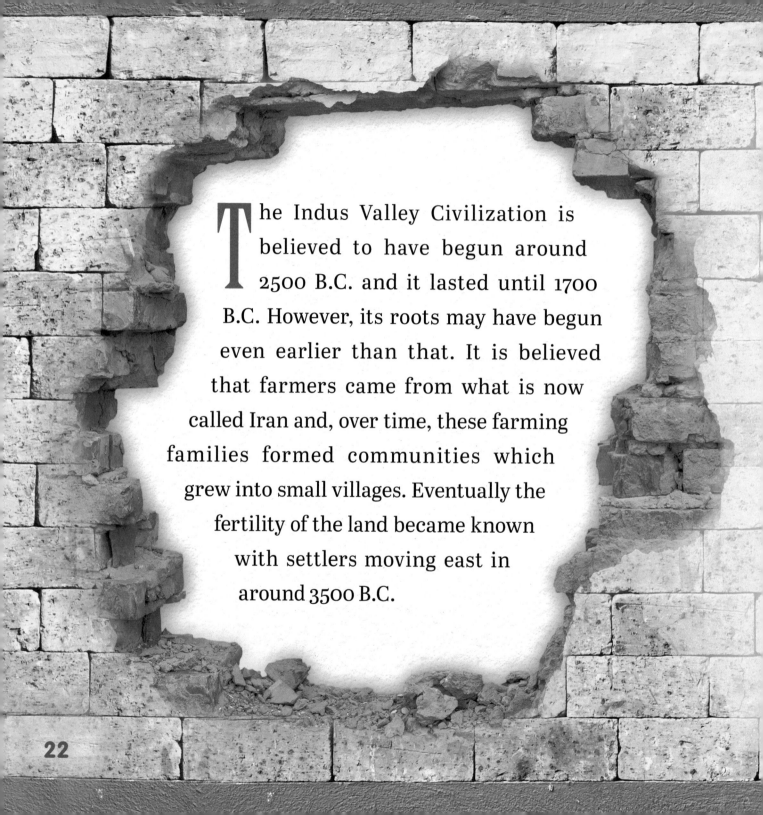

The Indus Valley Civilization is believed to have begun around 2500 B.C. and it lasted until 1700 B.C. However, its roots may have begun even earlier than that. It is believed that farmers came from what is now called Iran and, over time, these farming families formed communities which grew into small villages. Eventually the fertility of the land became known with settlers moving east in around 3500 B.C.

Khyber Pass

HINDU KUSH

Indus River

Harappa

Mohenjo-daro

Indus Valley Civilization

Brahmaputra River

HIMALAYAS

Thar Desert

Ganges River

Arabian Sea

Bay of Bengal

INDIAN OCEAN

N
W · E
S

MOHENJO-DARO RUINS IN LARKANA, PAKISTAN

24

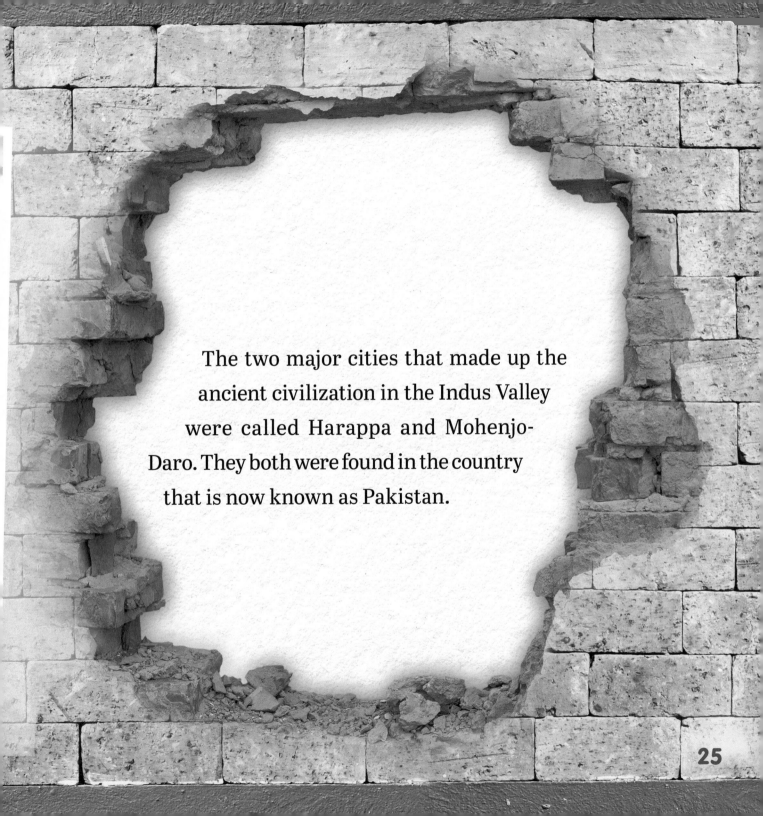

The two major cities that made up the ancient civilization in the Indus Valley were called Harappa and Mohenjo-Daro. They both were found in the country that is now known as Pakistan.

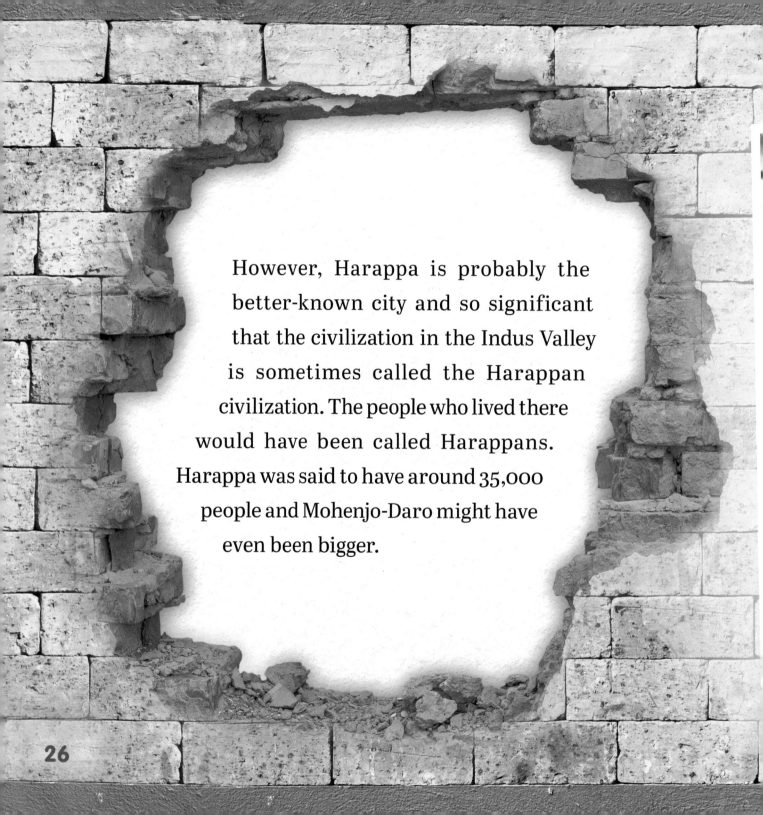

However, Harappa is probably the better-known city and so significant that the civilization in the Indus Valley is sometimes called the Harappan civilization. The people who lived there would have been called Harappans. Harappa was said to have around 35,000 people and Mohenjo-Daro might have even been bigger.

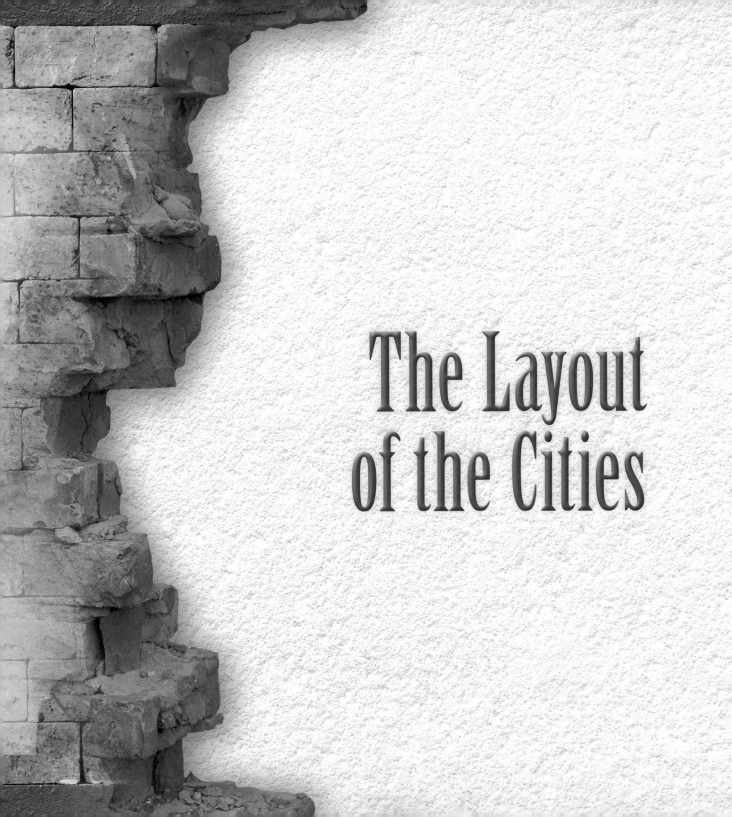

The Layout
of the Cities

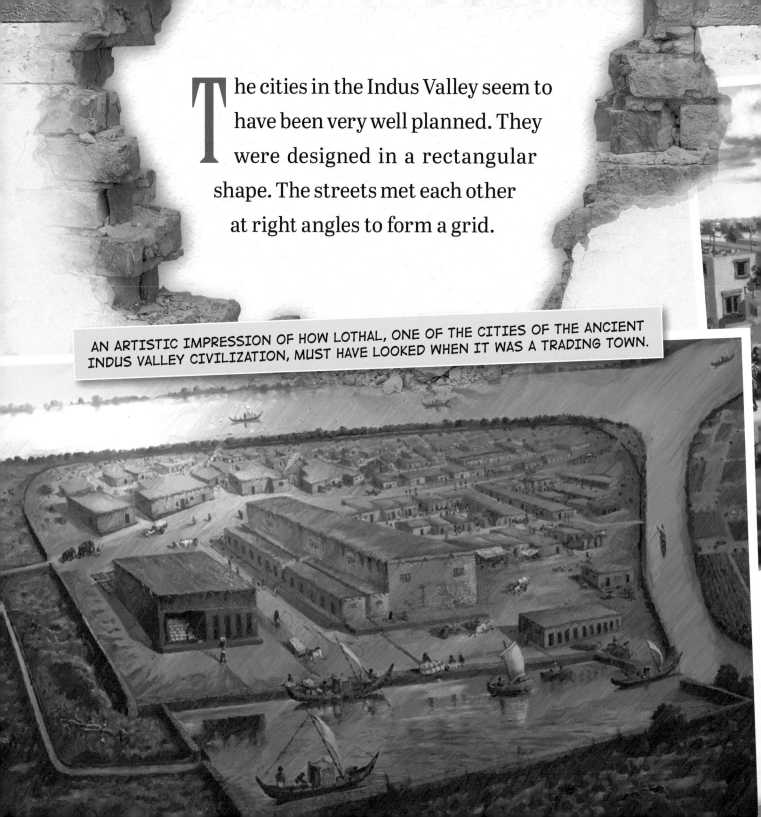

T he cities in the Indus Valley seem to have been very well planned. They were designed in a rectangular shape. The streets met each other at right angles to form a grid.

AN ARTISTIC IMPRESSION OF HOW LOTHAL, ONE OF THE CITIES OF THE ANCIENT INDUS VALLEY CIVILIZATION, MUST HAVE LOOKED WHEN IT WAS A TRADING TOWN.

Many shops would line these streets and each city was known to have a place set up as a grand market. As if to boast their prosperity, the largest structure in the city is said to have been the granaries.

A LOCAL MERCHANT WEIGHS BREAD WHILE TRADERS WAIT TO SELL THEIR GOODS.

BRICKS WALL IN THE EXCAVATED SITE OF HARAPPAN
CIVILIZATION AT DHOLAVIRA, GUJARAT, INDIA

To provide protection from possible attacks, the cities were surrounded by a brick wall and there was a citadel to keep out invaders. Harappans could hide inside the city for protection.

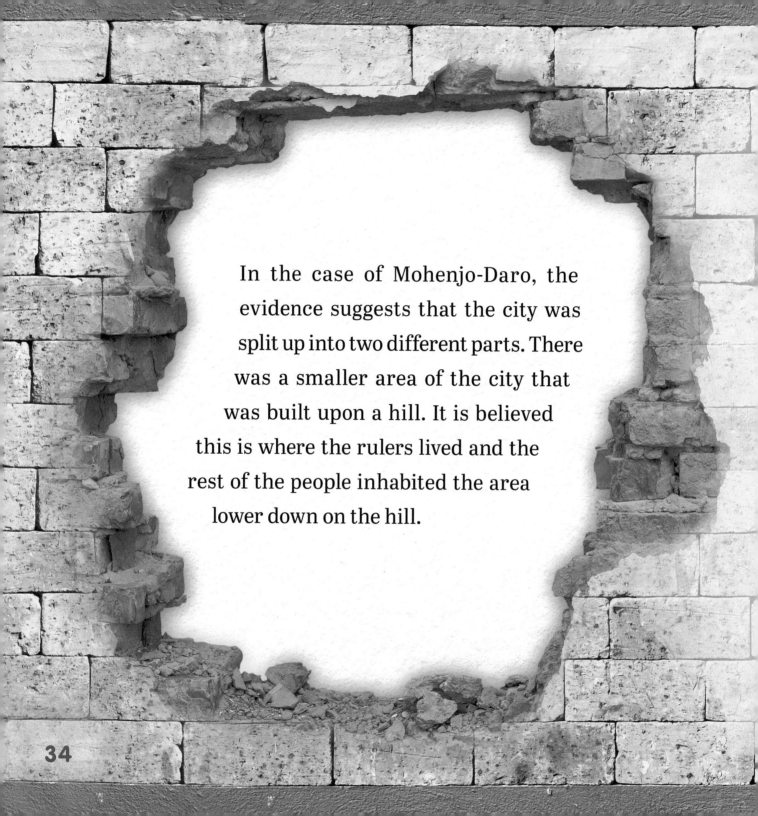

In the case of Mohenjo-Daro, the evidence suggests that the city was split up into two different parts. There was a smaller area of the city that was built upon a hill. It is believed this is where the rulers lived and the rest of the people inhabited the area lower down on the hill.

UPPER CITY

LOWER CITY

MOHENJO-DARO WAS SPLIT UP INTO TWO DIFFERENT PARTS.

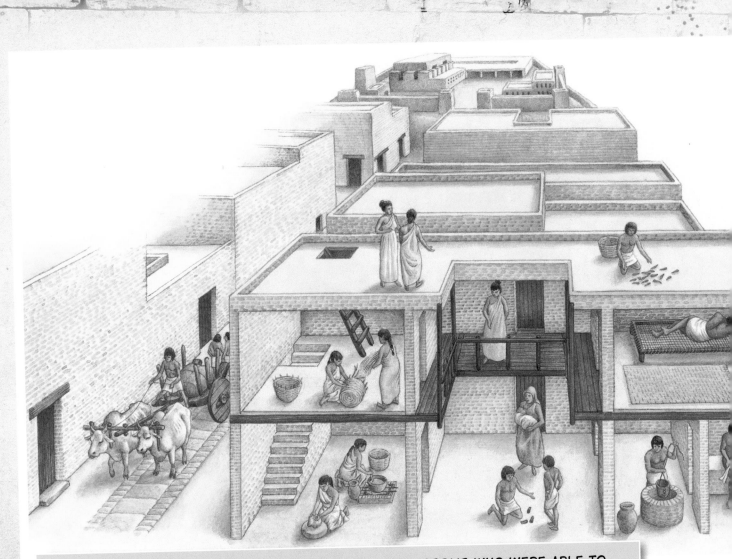

THE INDUS VALLEY CIVILIZATION HAD EXCELLENT MASONS WHO WERE ABLE TO CONSTRUCT LOAD-BEARING BRICK STRUCTURES UP TO TWO STORIES EFFORTLESSLY.

Remarkably, even the houses for common people were often made of brick. Some of the houses seem to have been a few stories high.

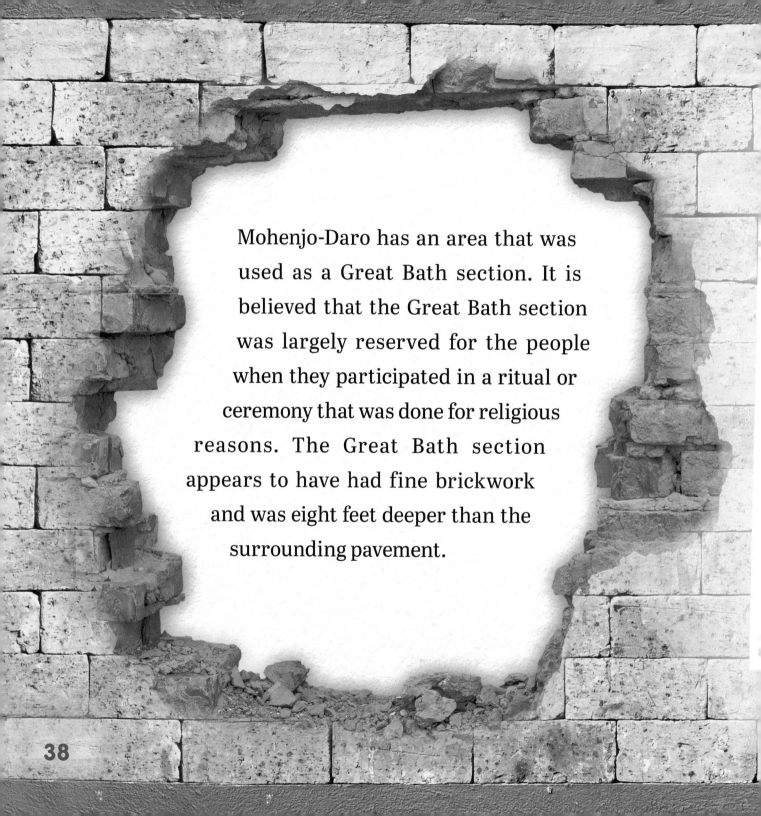

Mohenjo-Daro has an area that was used as a Great Bath section. It is believed that the Great Bath section was largely reserved for the people when they participated in a ritual or ceremony that was done for religious reasons. The Great Bath section appears to have had fine brickwork and was eight feet deeper than the surrounding pavement.

MOHENJO-DARO ARCHAEOLOGICAL UNESCO
WORLD HERITAGE VIEW OF GREAT BATH

THE BATHROOM-TOILET STRUCTURE OF
HOUSES DURING THE INDUS CIVILIZATION

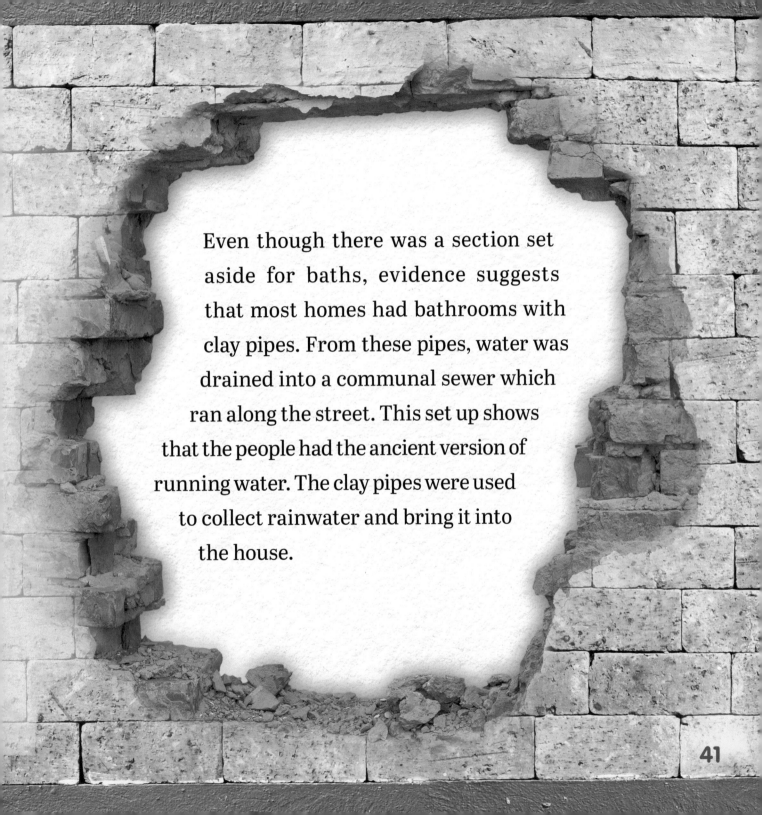

Even though there was a section set aside for baths, evidence suggests that most homes had bathrooms with clay pipes. From these pipes, water was drained into a communal sewer which ran along the street. This set up shows that the people had the ancient version of running water. The clay pipes were used to collect rainwater and bring it into the house.

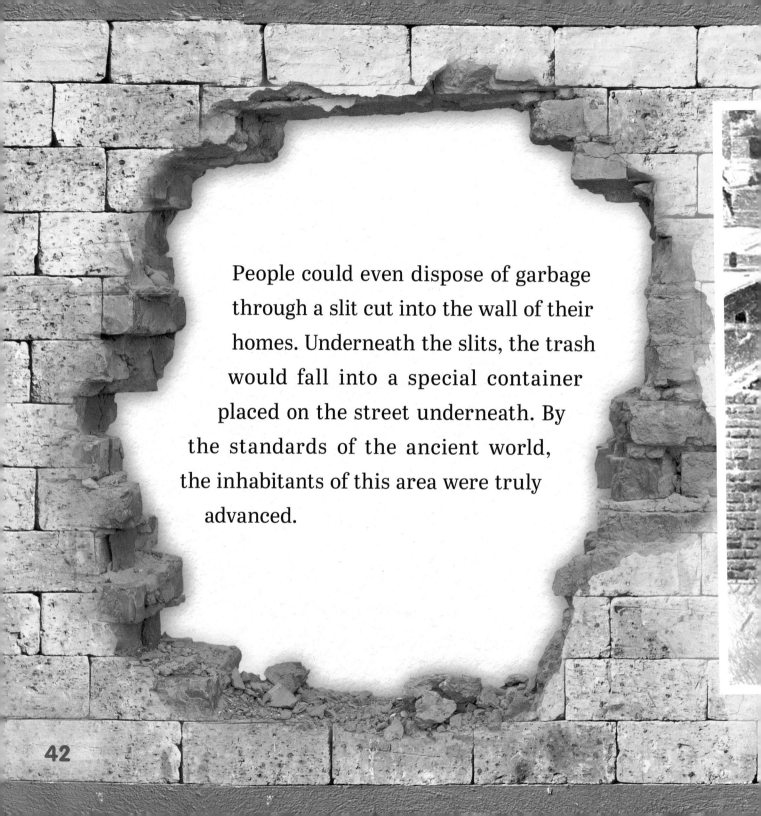

People could even dispose of garbage through a slit cut into the wall of their homes. Underneath the slits, the trash would fall into a special container placed on the street underneath. By the standards of the ancient world, the inhabitants of this area were truly advanced.

BY THE STANDARDS OF THE ANCIENT WORLD, THE INHABITANTS OF MOHENJO-DARO WERE TRULY ADVANCED.

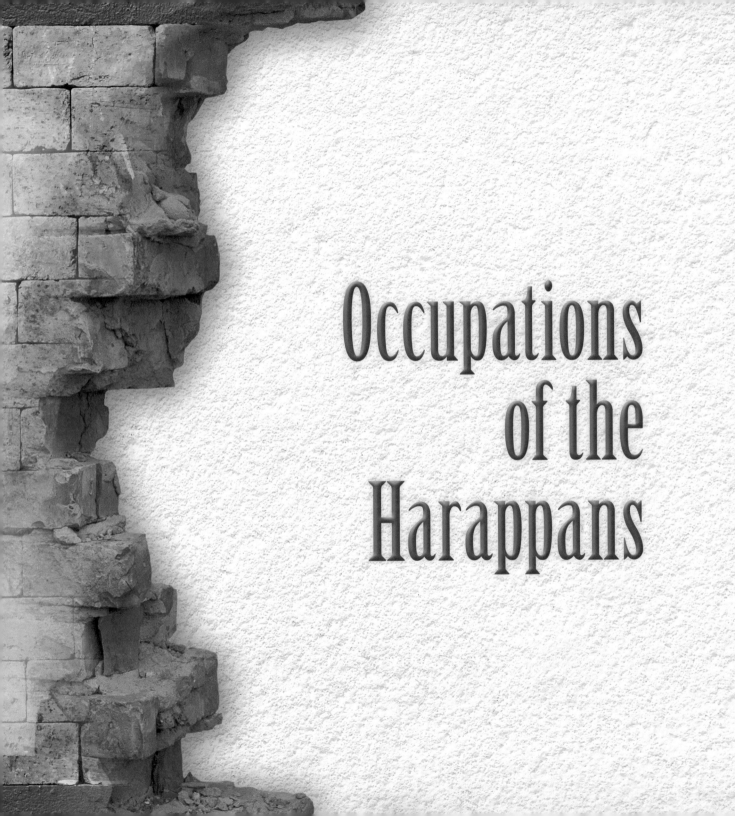

Occupations
of the
Harappans

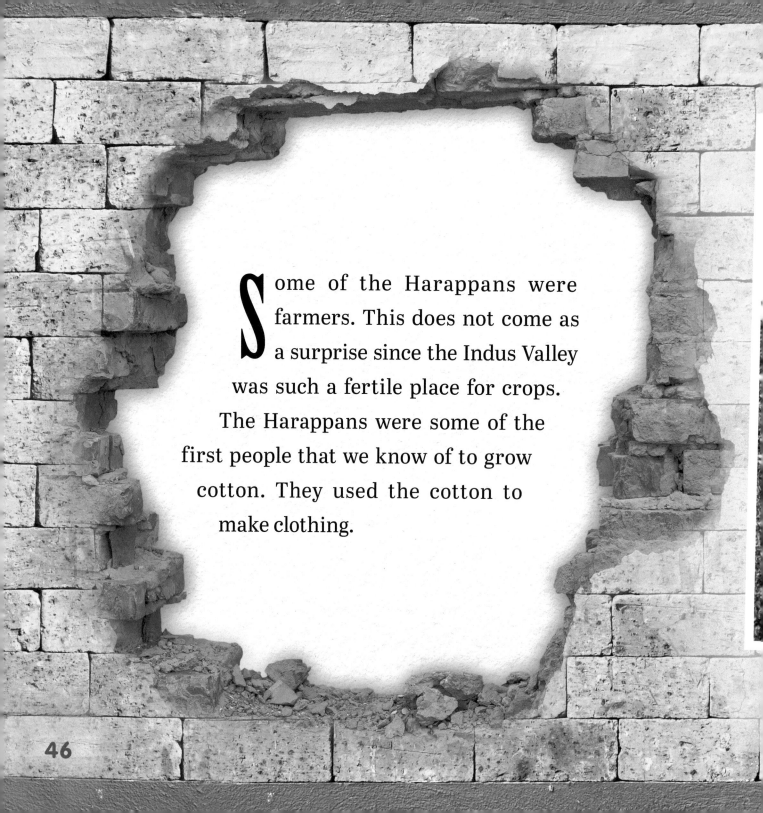

Some of the Harappans were farmers. This does not come as a surprise since the Indus Valley was such a fertile place for crops. The Harappans were some of the first people that we know of to grow cotton. They used the cotton to make clothing.

THE HARAPPANS WERE SOME OF THE FIRST PEOPLE TO GROW COTTON.

THE HARAPPANS GREW MANY KINDS OF CROPS.

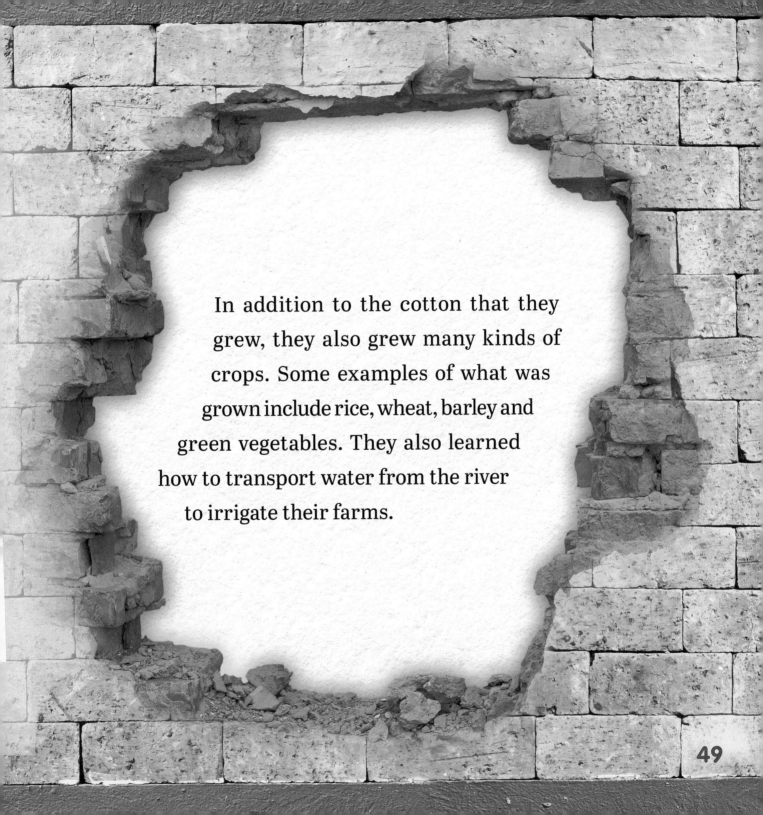

In addition to the cotton that they grew, they also grew many kinds of crops. Some examples of what was grown include rice, wheat, barley and green vegetables. They also learned how to transport water from the river to irrigate their farms.

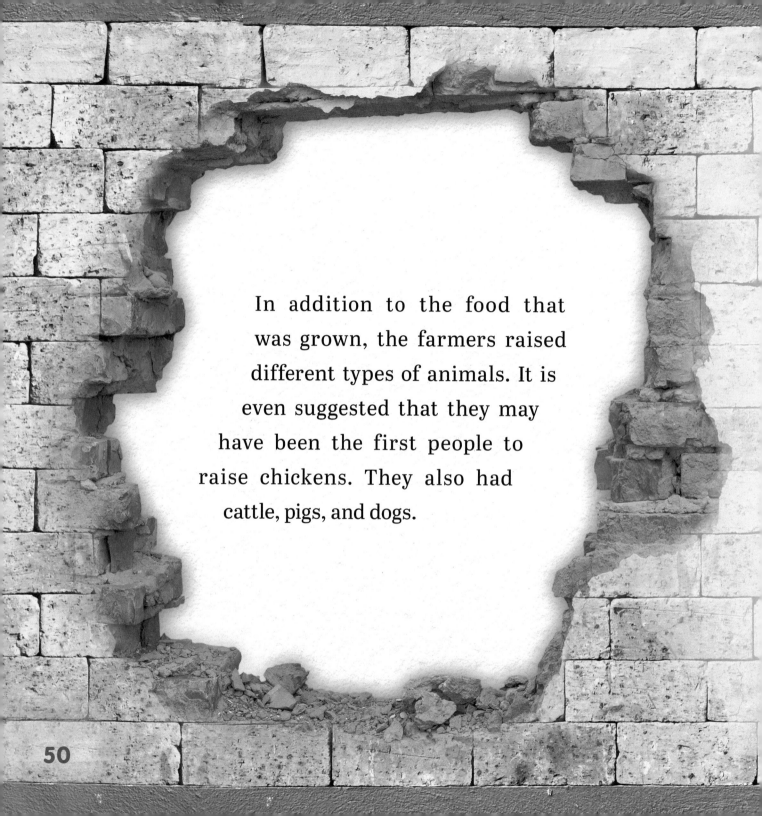

In addition to the food that was grown, the farmers raised different types of animals. It is even suggested that they may have been the first people to raise chickens. They also had cattle, pigs, and dogs.

THE HARAPPANS RAISED DIFFERENT TYPES OF ANIMALS.

GRANARY IN THE INDUS VALLEY

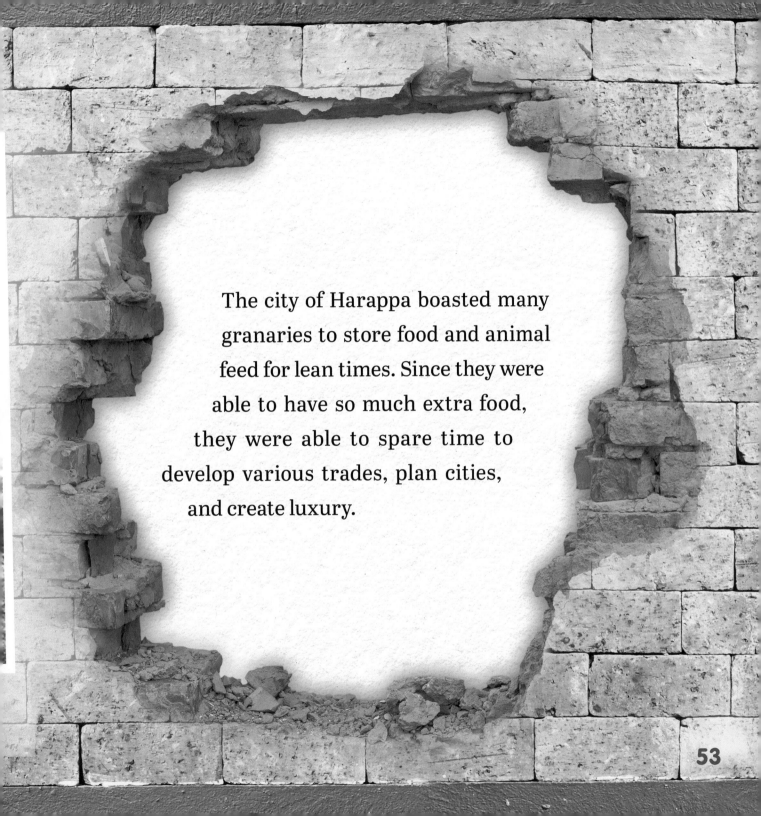

The city of Harappa boasted many granaries to store food and animal feed for lean times. Since they were able to have so much extra food, they were able to spare time to develop various trades, plan cities, and create luxury.

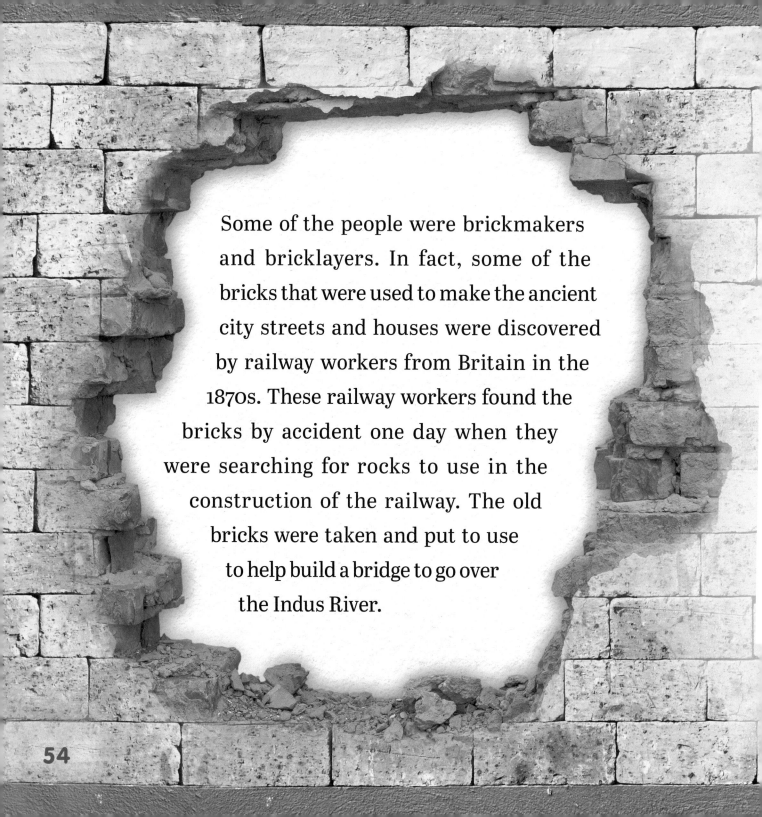

Some of the people were brickmakers and bricklayers. In fact, some of the bricks that were used to make the ancient city streets and houses were discovered by railway workers from Britain in the 1870s. These railway workers found the bricks by accident one day when they were searching for rocks to use in the construction of the railway. The old bricks were taken and put to use to help build a bridge to go over the Indus River.

ROAD AND BRICK WALL OF ANCIENT CITY RUINS OF
HARAPPA CIVILIZATION IN DHOLAVIRA, GUJARAT, INDIA

COLLECTION OF HARAPPA POTTERY FROM THE INDUS
VALLEY CIVILIZATION AT MOHENJO–DARO, PAKISTAN.

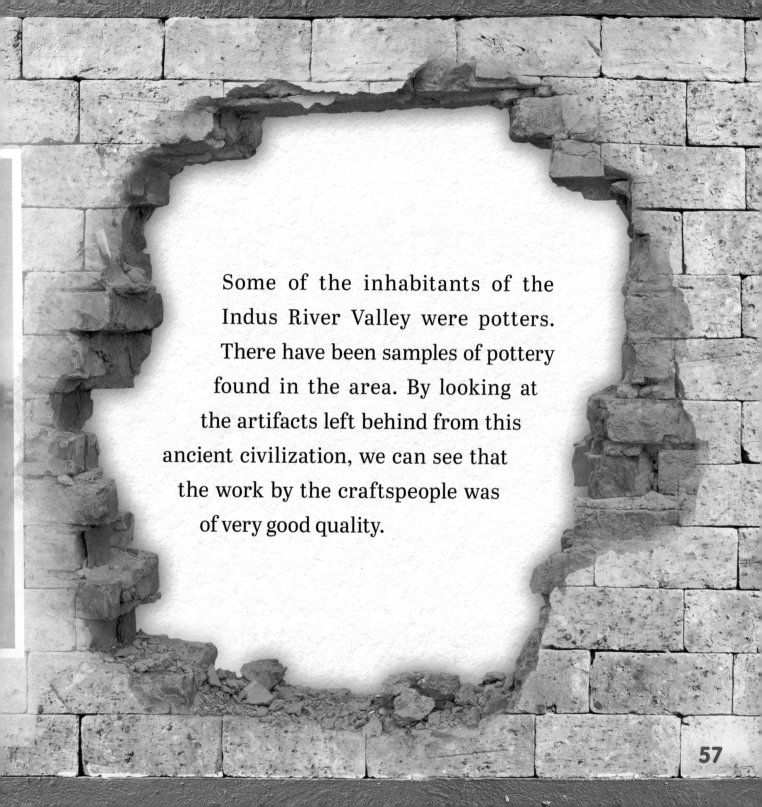

Some of the inhabitants of the Indus River Valley were potters. There have been samples of pottery found in the area. By looking at the artifacts left behind from this ancient civilization, we can see that the work by the craftspeople was of very good quality.

THE DANCING GIRL AND PRIEST-KING POTTERY
SCULPTURES ARE MADE WITH SUN-FIRED CLAY.

In addition to vases, bowls and other dishes, the craftspeople made little figurines. The material that was used was terra-cotta which is clay that has been baked. These terra-cotta figurines included replicas that resembled animals and people.

TERRACOTTA TOYS OF INDUS VALLEY CIVILIZATION FOUND BY ARCHAEOLOGICAL SURVEY OF INDIA AT LOTHAL, GUJARAT

All the dishes that were made were also decorated with great detail. Some of the figurines were used as toys.

Some of the people also spent time making tools and weapons. The materials that were used to make these items were bronze, copper and lead.

COPPER IMPLEMENTS SPEAR BLADES FROM THE INDUS VALLEY CIVILIZATION

COLLECTION OF BLADES FROM THE INDUS VALLEY CIVILIZATION AT MOHENJO-DARO, PAKISTAN.

Some items that were found were knives and spears.

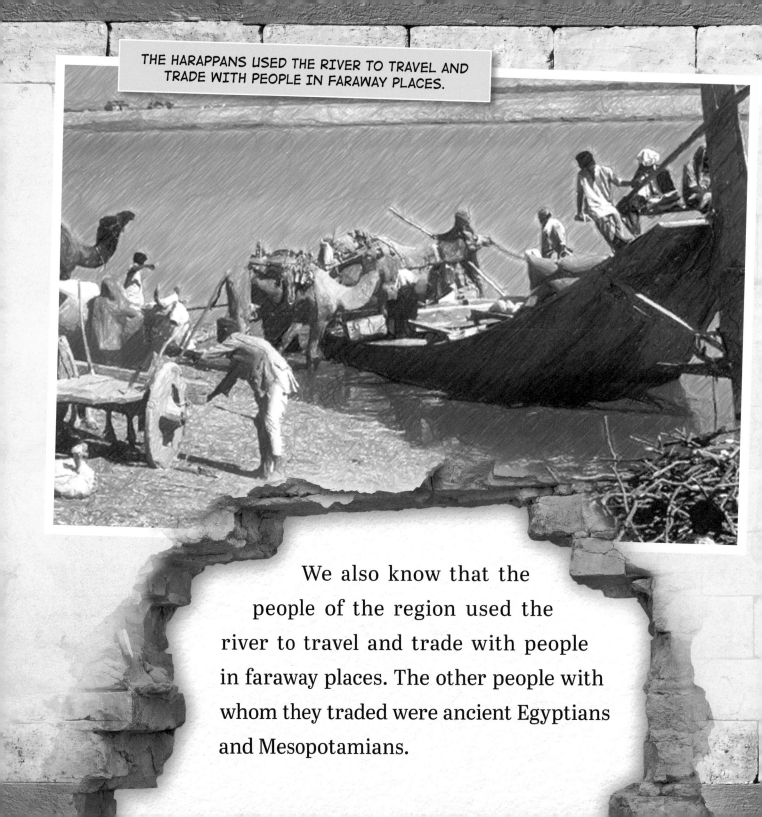

We also know that the people of the region used the river to travel and trade with people in faraway places. The other people with whom they traded were ancient Egyptians and Mesopotamians.

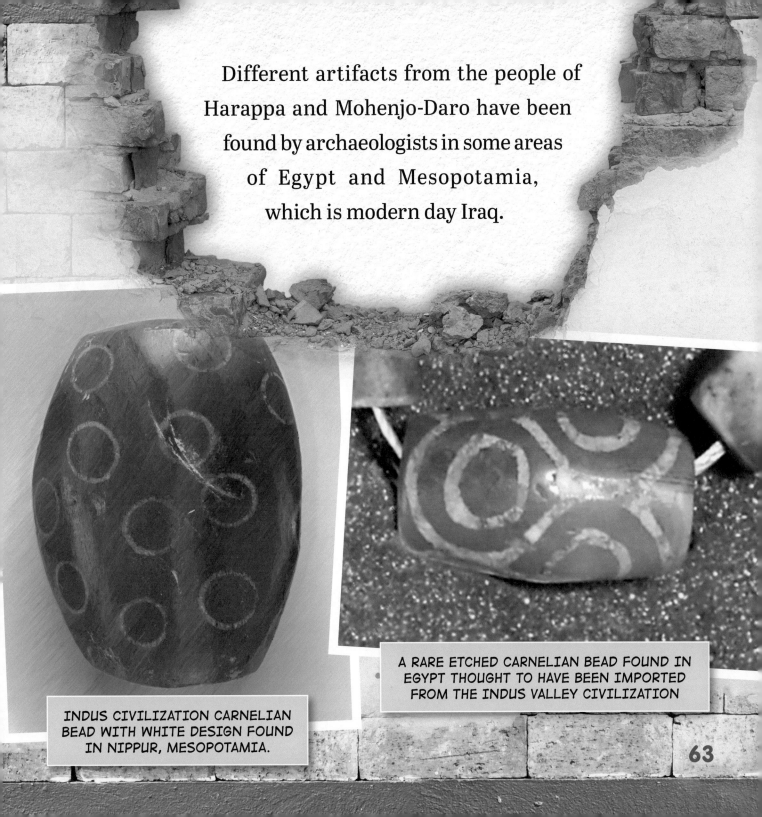

Different artifacts from the people of Harappa and Mohenjo-Daro have been found by archaeologists in some areas of Egypt and Mesopotamia, which is modern day Iraq.

INDUS CIVILIZATION CARNELIAN BEAD WITH WHITE DESIGN FOUND IN NIPPUR, MESOPOTAMIA.

A RARE ETCHED CARNELIAN BEAD FOUND IN EGYPT THOUGHT TO HAVE BEEN IMPORTED FROM THE INDUS VALLEY CIVILIZATION

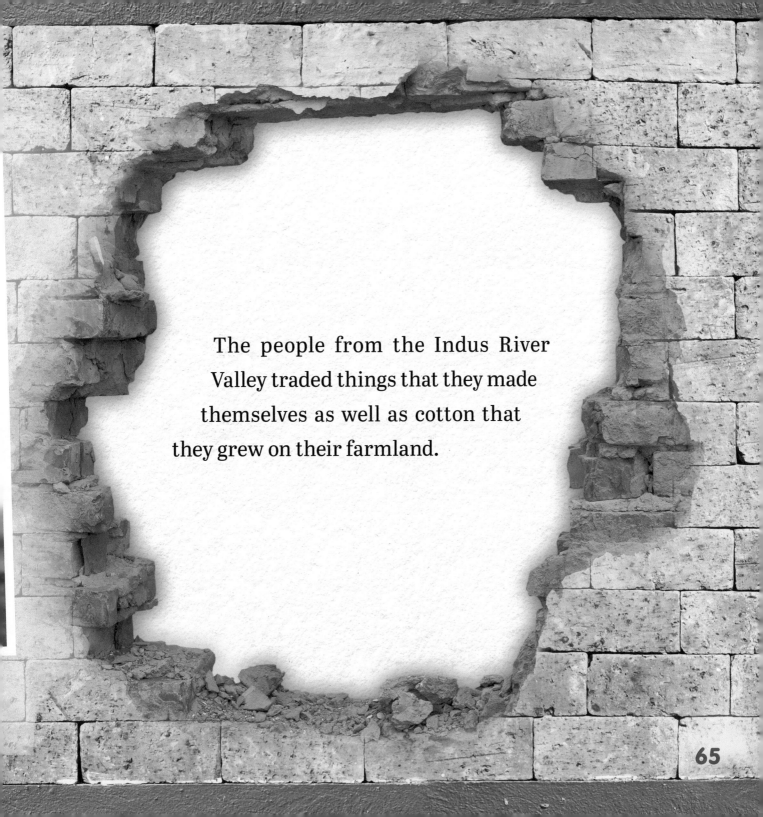

The people from the Indus River Valley traded things that they made themselves as well as cotton that they grew on their farmland.

When the people from Harappa and Mohenjo-Daro traveled to trade, in addition to their goods, they carried their seals.

THE PASHUPATI SEAL, SHOWING A SEATED AND POSSIBLY TRICEPHALIC FIGURE SURROUNDED BY ANIMALS.

Not only has there been evidence of artifacts of the people of the Indus River Valley Region being discovered in Egypt and Mesopotamia, there have been certain gemstones found in the Indus River Valley that are not originally from the valley. This shows that the people both traded their goods afar and returned with goods themselves.

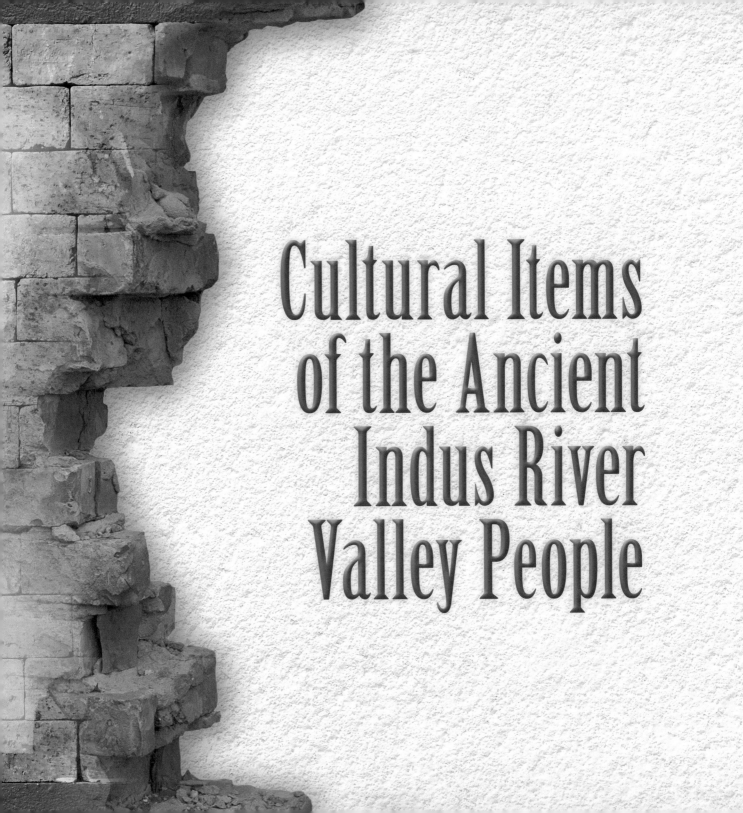

Cultural Items of the Ancient Indus River Valley People

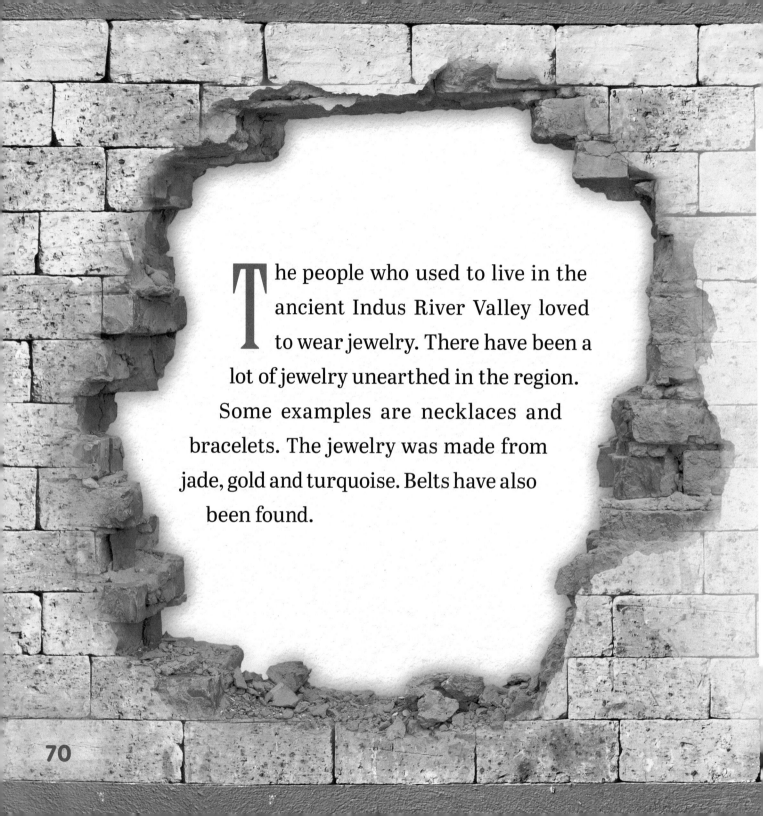

The people who used to live in the ancient Indus River Valley loved to wear jewelry. There have been a lot of jewelry unearthed in the region. Some examples are necklaces and bracelets. The jewelry was made from jade, gold and turquoise. Belts have also been found.

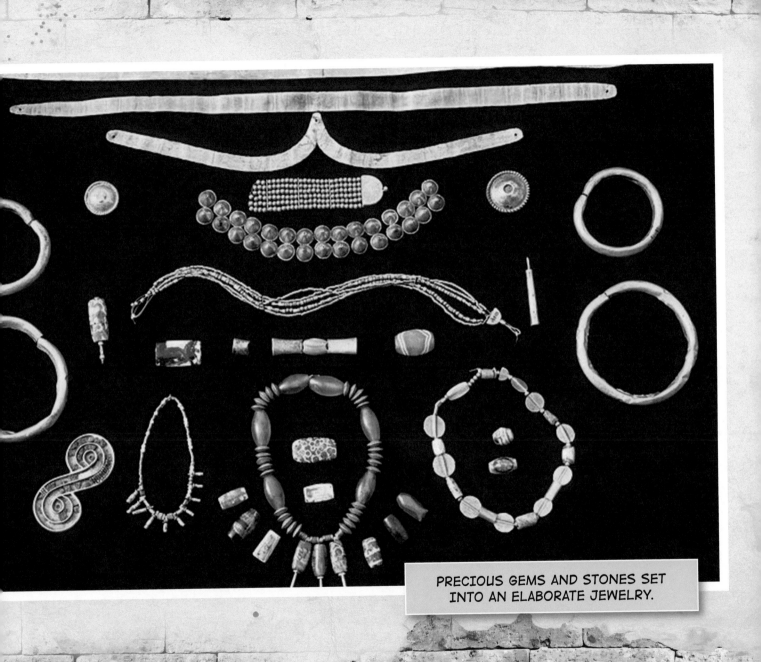

PRECIOUS GEMS AND STONES SET
INTO AN ELABORATE JEWELRY.

In addition, archaeologists have found samples of stamps and seals that were made from stone. The images of animals, such as elephants, rhinoceroses and bulls have been found carved into the seals. Some of the seals have writing engraved into them.

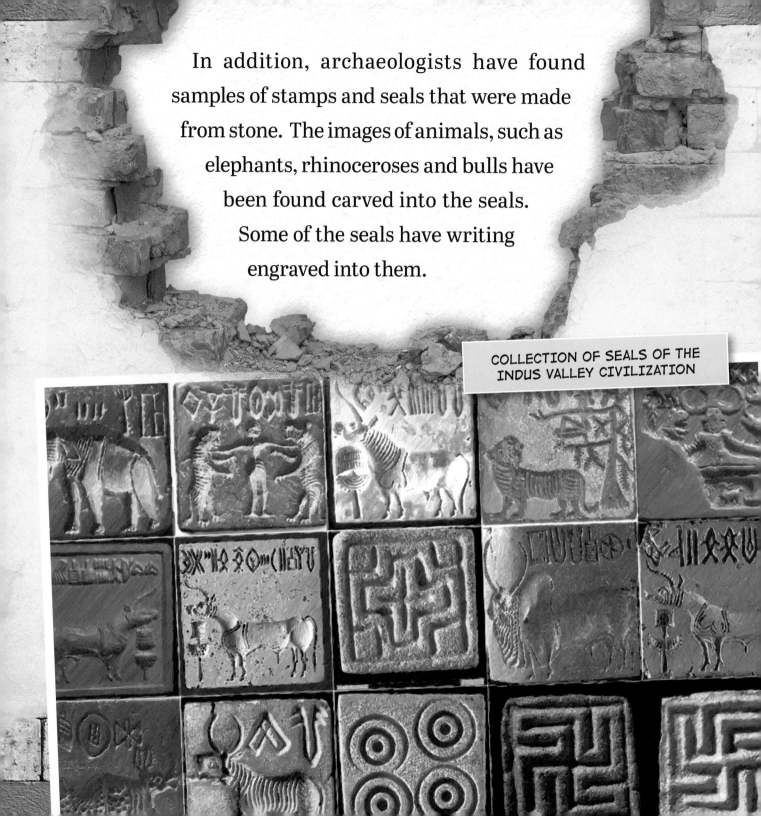

COLLECTION OF SEALS OF THE INDUS VALLEY CIVILIZATION

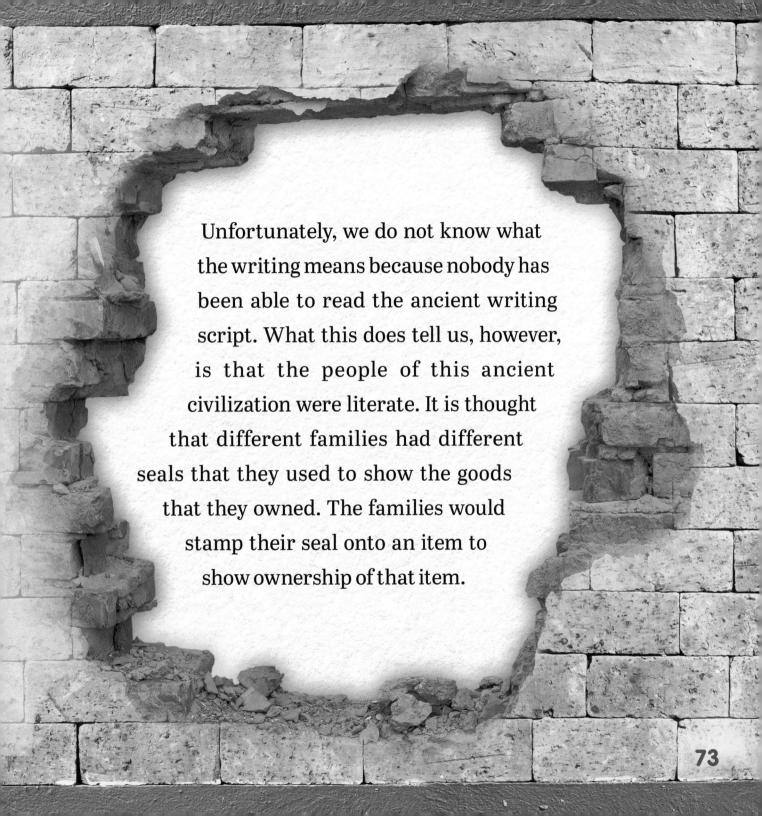

Unfortunately, we do not know what the writing means because nobody has been able to read the ancient writing script. What this does tell us, however, is that the people of this ancient civilization were literate. It is thought that different families had different seals that they used to show the goods that they owned. The families would stamp their seal onto an item to show ownership of that item.

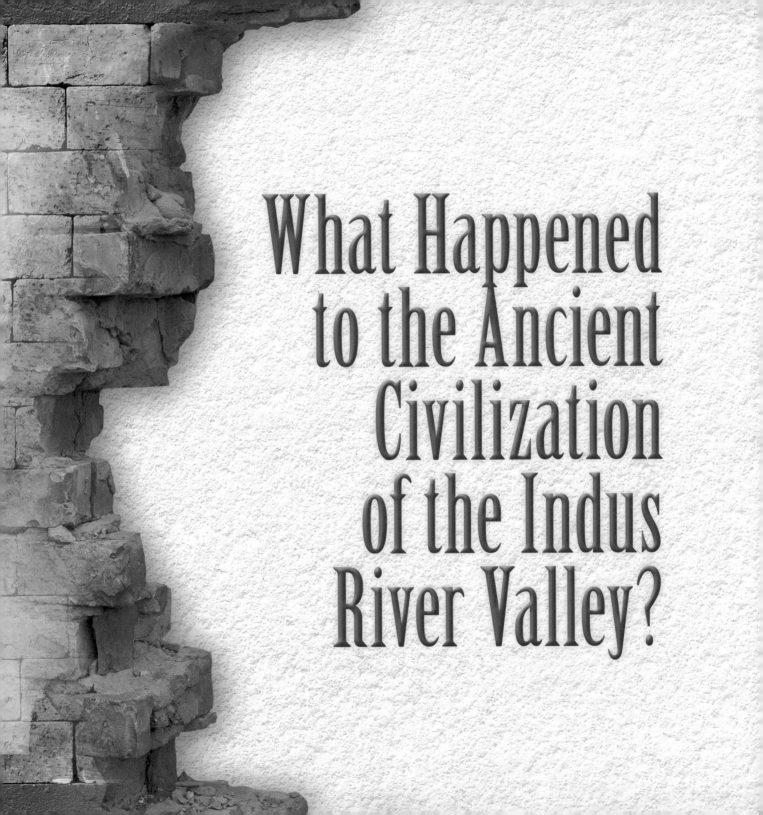

What Happened to the Ancient Civilization of the Indus River Valley?

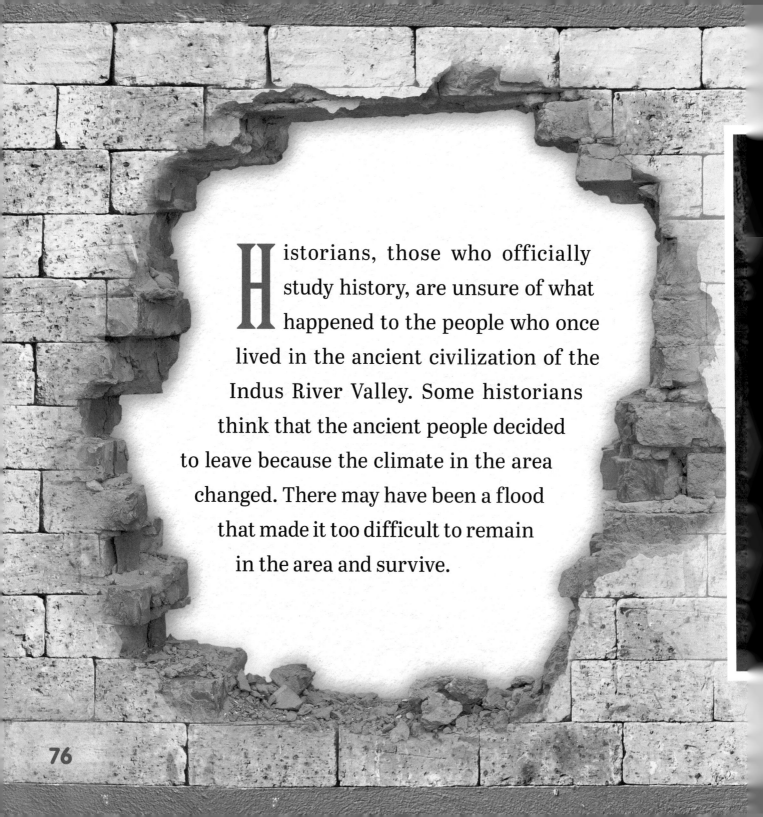

Historians, those who officially study history, are unsure of what happened to the people who once lived in the ancient civilization of the Indus River Valley. Some historians think that the ancient people decided to leave because the climate in the area changed. There may have been a flood that made it too difficult to remain in the area and survive.

A DIORAMA OF THE ANCIENT CIVILIZATION OF THE INDUS RIVER VALLEY.

SOME HISTORIANS SUSPECT THAT THE PEOPLE
WERE INVADED AND WERE FORCED TO LEAVE.

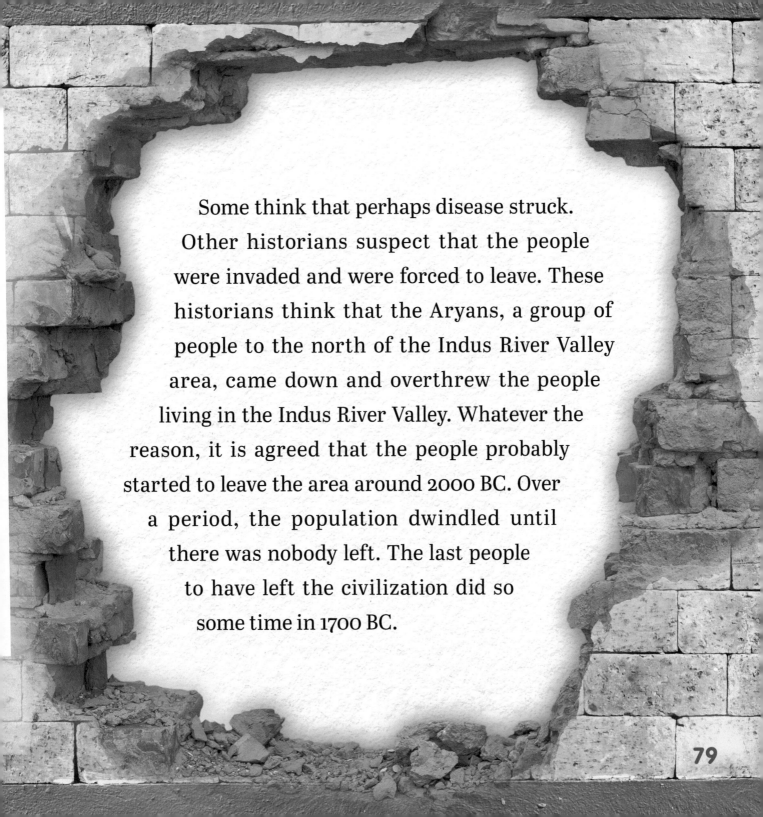

Some think that perhaps disease struck. Other historians suspect that the people were invaded and were forced to leave. These historians think that the Aryans, a group of people to the north of the Indus River Valley area, came down and overthrew the people living in the Indus River Valley. Whatever the reason, it is agreed that the people probably started to leave the area around 2000 BC. Over a period, the population dwindled until there was nobody left. The last people to have left the civilization did so some time in 1700 BC.

Although we may never know exactly why the people left their great civilization, archaeologists have been able to find a lot of artifacts from the people. It was in 1920 that excavations were started in the area. The examples of the remnants found show the talent and handiwork of the people.

INDUS VALLEY ARTIFACTS

Thanks to the ingenuity of the people, and the bounty of the Indus River Valley, the members of this ancient civilization lived in luxury during their time. The items that have been unearthed and the evidence of the archeological findings show that the people were prosperous.

INDUS RIVER IN LEH, LADAKH, INDIA

Visit

www.speedypublishing.com

To view and download free content
on your favorite subject and browse
our catalog of new and exciting
books for readers of all ages.